Step-by-Step, Practical Recipes Meat Eats: Contents

Beef

Beef is a very versatile meat that can work with a wide selection of ingredients, making it hard to resist!

Lamb

Fresh lamb is a succulent meat that is perfect roasted with herbs or slow cooked with a variety of fresh vegetables.

Pork

There are so many things that can be done with pork. Try all of these recipes to discover your favourite!

FLAME TREE has been creating family-friendly, classic and beginner recipes for our bestselling cookbooks for over 20 years now. Our mission is to offer you a wide range of expert-tested dishes, while providing clear images of the final dish so that you can match it to your own results. We hope you enjoy this super selection of recipes – there are plenty more to try! Titles in this series include:

Cupcakes • Slow Cooker • Curries Soups & Starters • Baking & Breads Cooking on a Budget • Winter Warmers Party Cakes • Meat Eats • Party Food Chocolate • Sweet Treats

www.flametreepublishing.com

Cornish Pasties

INGREDIENTS

Makes 8

For the pastry:

350 g/12 oz self-raising flour
75 g/3 oz butter or margarine
75 g/3 oz lard or white vegetable fat
salt and freshly ground black pepper

For the filling:

550 g/1¼ lb braising steak, chopped
   very finely
1 large onion, peeled and
   finely chopped
1 large potato, peeled and diced
200 g/7 oz swede, peeled and diced
3 tbsp Worcestershire sauce
1 small egg, beaten, to glaze

To garnish:

tomato slices or wedges
sprigs of fresh parsley

1   Preheat the oven to 180°C/350°F/Gas Mark 4, about 15 minutes before required. To make the pastry, sift the flour into a large bowl and add the fats, chopped into little pieces. Rub the fats and flour together until the mixture resembles coarse breadcrumbs. Season to taste with salt and pepper and mix again.

2   Add about 2 tablespoons of cold water, a little at a time, and mix until the mixture comes together to form a firm but pliable dough. Turn onto a lightly floured surface, knead until smooth, then wrap and chill in the refrigerator.

3   To make the filling, put the braising steak in a large bowl with the onion. Add the potatoes and swede to the bowl together with the Worcestershire sauce and salt and pepper. Mix well.

4   Divide the dough into 8 balls and roll each ball into a circle about 25.5 cm/10 inches across. Divide the filling between the circles of pastry. Wet the edge of the pastry, then fold over the filling. Pinch the edges to seal.

5   Transfer the pasties to a lightly oiled baking sheet. Make a couple of small holes in each pasty and brush with beaten egg. Cook in the preheated oven for 15 minutes, remove and brush again with the egg. Return to the oven for a further 15–20 minutes until golden. Cool slightly, garnish with tomato and parsley and serve.

TASTY TIP

The shortcrust pastry for these pasties is made with self-raising flour, which gives it a softer, lighter texture.

2

3

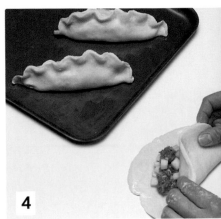

4

Chilli Con Carne with Crispy-skinned Potatoes

INGREDIENTS

Serves 4

2 tbsp vegetable oil, plus extra
　for brushing
1 large onion, peeled and
　finely chopped
1 garlic clove, peeled and
　finely chopped
1 red chilli, deseeded and
　finely chopped
450 g/1 lb chuck steak, finely
　chopped, or lean beef mince
1 tbsp chilli powder
400 g can chopped tomatoes
2 tbsp tomato purée
400 g can red kidney beans, drained
　and rinsed
4 large baking potatoes
coarse salt and freshly ground
　black pepper

To serve:

ready-made guacamole
soured cream

1 Preheat the oven to 150°C/300°F/Gas Mark 2. Heat the oil in a large flameproof casserole and add the onion. Cook gently for 10 minutes until soft and lightly browned. Add the garlic and chilli and cook briefly. Increase the heat. Add the chuck steak or lean mince and cook for a further 10 minutes, stirring occasionally, until browned.

2 Add the chilli powder and stir well. Cook for about 2 minutes, then add the chopped tomatoes and tomato purée. Bring slowly to the boil. Cover and cook in the preheated oven for 1½ hours. Remove from the oven and stir in the kidney beans. Return to the oven for a further 15 minutes.

3 Meanwhile, brush a little vegetable oil all over the potatoes and rub on some coarse salt. Put the potatoes in the oven alongside the chilli.

4 Remove the chilli and potatoes from the oven. Cut a cross in each potato, then squeeze to open slightly and season to taste with salt and pepper. Serve with the chilli, guacamole and soured cream.

2

2

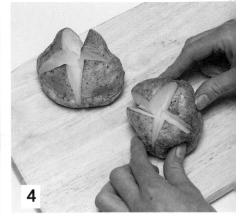

4

Pan-fried Steaks with Saffron Potatoes & Roast Tomatoes

INGREDIENTS

Serves 4

700 g/1½ lb new potatoes, halved

few strands of saffron

300 ml/½ pint vegetable
  or beef stock

1 small onion, peeled and
  finely chopped

75 g/3 oz butter

salt and freshly ground black pepper

2 tsp balsamic vinegar

2 tbsp olive oil

1 tsp caster sugar

8 plum tomatoes, halved

4 boneless sirloin steaks, each
  weighing 225 g/8 oz

2 tbsp freshly chopped parsley

HELPFUL HINT

When cooking steak timing depends on the thickness rather than the weight of the steak. As a rough guide a 2 cm/¾ inch thick steak will take about 2 minutes on each side for rare, 3–4 minutes on each side for medium and 6–7 minutes on each side for well-done.

1 Cook the potatoes in boiling salted water for 8 minutes and drain well. Return the potatoes to the saucepan along with the saffron, stock, onion and 25 g/1 oz of the butter. Season to taste with salt and pepper and simmer, uncovered for 10 minutes until the potatoes are tender.

2 Meanwhile, preheat the grill to medium. Mix together the vinegar, olive oil, sugar and seasoning. Arrange the tomatoes cut-side up in a foil-lined grill pan and drizzle over the dressing. Grill for 12–15 minutes, basting occasionally, until tender.

3 Melt the remaining butter in a frying pan. Add the steaks and cook for 4–8 minutes to taste and depending on thickness.

4 Arrange the potatoes and tomatoes in the centre of 4 serving plates. Top with the steaks along with any pan juices. Sprinkle over the parsley and serve immediately.

Pan-fried Beef with Creamy Mushrooms

INGREDIENTS

Serves 4

225 g/8 oz shallots, peeled
2 garlic cloves, peeled
2 tbsp olive oil
4 medallions of beef
4 plum tomatoes
125 g/4 oz flat mushrooms
3 tbsp brandy
150 ml/¼ pint red wine
salt and freshly ground black pepper
4 tbsp double cream

To serve:
baby new potatoes
freshly cooked green beans

1 Cut the shallots in half if large, then chop the garlic. Heat the oil in a large frying pan and cook the shallots for about 8 minutes, stirring occasionally, until almost softened. Add the garlic and beef and cook for 8–10 minutes, turning once during cooking until the meat is browned all over. Using a slotted spoon, transfer the beef to a plate and keep warm.

2 Rinse the tomatoes and cut into eighths, then wipe the mushrooms and slice. Add to the pan and cook for 5 minutes, stirring frequently until the mushrooms have softened.

3 Pour in the brandy and heat through. Draw the pan off the heat and carefully ignite. Allow the flames to subside. Pour in the wine, return to the heat and bring to the boil. Boil until reduced by one-third. Draw the pan off the heat, season to taste with salt and pepper, add the cream and stir.

4 Arrange the beef on serving plates and spoon over the sauce. Serve with baby new potatoes and a few green beans.

HELPFUL HINT

To prepare medallions of beef, buy a piece of fillet weighing approximately 700 g/1½ lb. Cut crosswise into 4 pieces.

1

2

3

Traditional Lasagne

INGREDIENTS

Serves 4

450 g/1 lb lean minced beef steak
175 g/6 oz pancetta or smoked
  streaky bacon, chopped
1 large onion, peeled and chopped
2 celery stalks, trimmed and chopped
125 g/4 oz button mushrooms, wiped
  and chopped
2 garlic cloves, peeled and chopped
90 g/3½ oz plain flour
300 ml/½ pint beef stock
1 tbsp freeze-dried mixed herbs
5 tbsp tomato purée
salt and freshly ground black pepper
75 g/3 oz butter
1 tsp English mustard powder
pinch of freshly grated nutmeg
900 ml/1½ pints milk
125 g/4 oz Parmesan cheese, grated
125 g/4 oz Cheddar cheese, grated
8–12 precooked lasagne sheets

To serve:
crusty bread
fresh green salad leaves

1 Preheat oven to 200°C/400°F/Gas Mark 6, 15 minutes before cooking. Cook the beef and pancetta in a large saucepan for 10 minutes, stirring to break up any lumps. Add the onion, celery and mushrooms and cook for 4 minutes, or until softened slightly.

2 Stir in the garlic and 1 tablespoon of the flour, then cook for 1 minute. Stir in the stock, herbs and tomato purée. Season to taste with salt and pepper. Bring to the boil, then cover, reduce the heat and simmer for 45 minutes.

3 Meanwhile, melt the butter in a small saucepan and stir in the remaining flour, mustard powder and nutmeg, until well blended. Cook for 2 minutes. Remove from the heat and gradually blend in the milk until smooth. Return to the heat and bring to the boil, stirring, until thickened. Gradually stir in half the Parmesan and Cheddar cheeses until melted. Season to taste.

4 Spoon half the meat mixture into the base of a large ovenproof dish. Top with a single layer of pasta. Spread over half the sauce and scatter with half the cheese. Repeat layers finishing with cheese. Bake in the preheated oven for 30 minutes, or until the pasta is cooked and the top is golden brown and bubbling. Serve immediately with crusty bread and a green salad.

2

3

4

Fillet Steaks with Tomato & Garlic Sauce

INGREDIENTS

Serves 4

700 g/1½ lb ripe tomatoes
2 garlic cloves
2 tbsp olive oil
2 tbsp freshly chopped basil
2 tbsp freshly chopped oregano
2 tbsp red wine
salt and freshly ground black pepper
75 g/3 oz pitted black olives, chopped
4 fillet steaks, about 175 g/6 oz each
  in weight
freshly cooked vegetables, to serve

1 Make a small cross on the top of each tomato and place in a large bowl. Cover with boiling water and leave for 2 minutes. Using a slotted spoon, remove the tomatoes and skin carefully. Repeat until all the tomatoes are skinned. Place on a chopping board, cut into quarters, remove the seeds and roughly chop, then reserve.

2 Peel and chop the garlic. Heat half the olive oil in a saucepan and cook the garlic for 30 seconds. Add the chopped tomatoes with the basil, oregano, red wine and season to taste with salt and pepper.

3 Bring to the boil then reduce the heat, cover and simmer for 15 minutes, stirring occasionally, or until the sauce is reduced and thickened. Stir the olives into the sauce and keep warm while cooking the steaks.

4 Meanwhile, lightly oil a griddle pan or heavy-based frying pan with the remaining olive oil and cook the steaks for 2 minutes on each side to seal. Continue to cook the steaks for a further 2–4 minutes, depending on personal preference. Serve the steaks immediately with the garlic sauce and freshly cooked vegetables.

HELPFUL HINT

Fillet steak should be a deep mahogany colour with a good marbling of fat. If the meat is bright red or if the fat is bright white the meat has not been aged properly and will probably be quite tough.

1

2

4

Spaghetti Bolognese

INGREDIENTS

Serves 4

1 carrot

2 celery stalks

1 onion

2 garlic cloves

450 g/1 lb lean minced beef steak

225 g/8 oz smoked streaky
  bacon, chopped

1 tbsp plain flour

150 ml/¼ pint red wine

379 g can chopped tomatoes

2 tbsp tomato purée

2 tsp dried mixed herbs

salt and freshly ground black pepper

pinch of sugar

350 g/12 oz spaghetti

sprigs of fresh oregano, to garnish

shavings of Parmesan cheese,
  to serve

TASTY TIP

This is an ideal sauce to use in a baked lasagne. Layer up the sauce with sheets of lasagne and top with a bechamel sauce and Parmesan cheese. Bake for 30–40 minutes in a preheated oven 190°C/375°F/Gas Mark 5, or until bubbling and the top is golden.

1　Peel and chop the carrot, trim and chop the celery, then peel and chop the onion and garlic. Heat a large non-stick frying pan and sauté the beef and bacon for 5–10 minutes, stirring occasionally, until browned. Add the prepared vegetables to the frying pan and cook for about 3 minutes, or until softened, stirring occasionally.

2　Add the flour and cook for 1 minute. Stir in the red wine, tomatoes, tomato purée, mixed herbs, seasoning to taste and sugar. Bring to the boil, then cover and simmer for 45 minutes, stirring occasionally.

3　Meanwhile, bring a large saucepan of lightly salted water to the boil and cook the spaghetti for 10–12 minutes, or until 'al dente'. Drain well and divide between 4 serving plates. Spoon over the sauce, garnish with a few sprigs of oregano and serve immediately with plenty of Parmesan shavings.

Roast Leg of Lamb & Boulangere Potatoes

INGREDIENTS

Serves 6

1.1 kg/2½ lb potatoes, peeled
1 large onion, peeled and finely sliced
salt and freshly ground black pepper
2 tbsp olive oil
50 g/2 oz butter
200 ml/7 fl oz lamb stock
100 ml/3½ fl oz milk
2 kg/4½ lb leg of lamb
2–3 sprigs of fresh rosemary
6 large garlic cloves, peeled
  and finely sliced
6 anchovy fillets, drained
extra sprigs of fresh rosemary,
  to garnish

FOOD FACT

Leg of lamb is one of the prime roasting joints and is known by its French name gigot in Scotland. It may weigh between 1.8–2.7 kg/ 4–6 lb, so ask for a small joint for this dish. Although home-produced lamb is at its best in the spring, there is a good supply all year round of imported New Zealand lamb.

1 Preheat the oven to 230°C/450°F/Gas Mark 8. Finely slice the potatoes – a mandolin is the best tool for this. Layer the potatoes with the onion in a large roasting tin, seasoning each layer with salt and pepper. Drizzle about 1 tablespoon of the olive oil over the potatoes and add the butter in small pieces. Pour in the lamb stock and milk. Set aside.

2 Make small incisions all over the lamb with the point of a small, sharp knife. Into each incision insert a small piece of rosemary, a sliver of garlic and a piece of anchovy fillet.

3 Drizzle the leg of lamb and its flavourings with the rest of the olive oil and season well. Place the meat directly onto a shelf in the preheated oven. Position the roasting tin of potatoes directly underneath to catch the juices during cooking. Roast for 15 minutes per 500 g/1 lb 2 oz (about 1 hour for a joint this size), reducing the oven temperature after 20 minutes to 200°C/400°F/Gas Mark 6.

4 When the lamb is cooked, remove from the oven and allow to rest for 10 minutes before carving. Meanwhile, increase the oven heat and cook the potatoes for a further 10–15 minutes to crisp up. Garnish with fresh rosemary sprigs and serve immediately with the lamb.

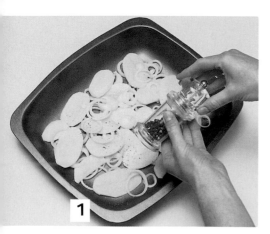

1

1

2

Lancashire Hotpot

INGREDIENTS

Serves 4

1 kg/2¼ lb middle end neck of lamb,
  divided into cutlets
2 tbsp vegetable oil
2 large onions, peeled and sliced
2 tsp plain flour
150 ml/¼ pint vegetable
  or lamb stock
700 g/1½ lb waxy potatoes, peeled
  and thickly sliced
salt and freshly ground black pepper
1 bay leaf
2 sprigs of fresh thyme
1 tbsp melted butter
2 tbsp freshly chopped herbs,
  to garnish
freshly cooked green beans, to serve

FOOD FACT

There are dozens of versions of this classic dish all claiming to be authentic. Some include lambs' kidneys to enrich the gravy, but whatever the ingredients, it is important to season well and to cook it slowly, so that the lamb is meltingly tender.

1 Preheat the oven to 170°C/325°F/Gas Mark 3. Trim any excess fat from the lamb cutlets. Heat the oil in a frying pan and brown the cutlets in batches for 3–4 minutes. Remove with a slotted spoon and reserve. Add the onions to the frying pan and cook for 6–8 minutes until softened and just beginning to colour, then remove and reserve.

2 Stir in the flour and cook for a few seconds, then gradually pour in the stock, stirring well, and bring to the boil. Remove from the heat.

3 Spread the base of a large casserole with half the potato slices. Top with half the onions and season well with salt and pepper. Arrange the browned meat in a layer. Season again and add the remaining onions, bay leaf and thyme. Pour in the remaining liquid from the onions and top with remaining potatoes so that they overlap in a single layer. Brush the potatoes with the melted butter and season again.

4 Cover the saucepan and cook in the preheated oven for 2 hours, uncovering for the last 30 minutes to allow the potatoes to brown. Garnish with chopped herbs and serve immediately with green beans.

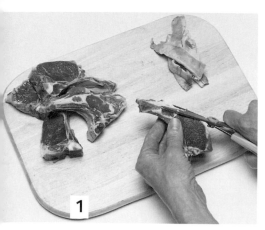

Shepherd's Pie

INGREDIENTS

Serves 4

2 tbsp vegetable or olive oil

1 onion, peeled and finely chopped

1 carrot, peeled and finely chopped

1 celery stalk, trimmed and
finely chopped

1 tbsp sprigs of fresh thyme

450 g/1 lb leftover roast lamb,
finely chopped

150 ml/¼ pint red wine

150 ml/¼ pint lamb or vegetable
stock or leftover gravy

2 tbsp tomato purée

salt and freshly ground black pepper

700 g/1½ lb potatoes, peeled and cut
into chunks

25 g/1 oz butter

6 tbsp milk

1 tbsp freshly chopped parsley

fresh herbs, to garnish

TASTY TIP

A traditional Shepherd's pie is always made from cold roast lamb, but it can be made with fresh minced lamb. Dry-fry 450 g/ 1 lb lean mince in a frying pan over a high heat until well-browned, then follow the recipe as before.

1 Preheat the oven to 200°C/400°F/Gas Mark 6, about 15 minutes before cooking. Heat the oil in a large saucepan and add the onion, carrot and celery. Cook over a medium heat for 8–10 minutes until softened and starting to brown.

2 Add the thyme and cook briefly, then add the cooked lamb, wine, stock and tomato purée. Season to taste with salt and pepper and simmer gently for 25–30 minutes until reduced and thickened. Remove from the heat to cool slightly and season again.

3 Meanwhile, boil the potatoes in plenty of salted water for 12–15 minutes until tender. Drain and return to the saucepan over a low heat to dry out. Remove from the heat and add the butter, milk and parsley. Mash until creamy, adding a little more milk if necessary. Adjust the seasoning.

4 Transfer the lamb mixture to a shallow ovenproof dish. Spoon the mash over the filling and spread evenly to cover completely. Fork the surface, place on a baking sheet, then cook in the preheated oven for 25–30 minutes until the potato topping is browned and the filling is piping hot. Garnish and serve.

2

3

4

Marinated Lamb Chops with Garlic Fried Potatoes

INGREDIENTS

Serves 4

4 thick lamb chump chops

3 tbsp olive oil

550 g/1¼ lb potatoes, peeled and cut
   into 1 cm/½ inch dice

6 unpeeled garlic cloves

mixed salad or freshly cooked
   vegetables, to serve

For the marinade:

1 small bunch of fresh thyme,
   leaves removed

1 tbsp freshly chopped rosemary

1 tsp salt

2 garlic cloves, peeled and crushed

rind and juice of 1 lemon

2 tbsp olive oil

TASTY TIP

Marinating the chops not only adds flavour, but tenderises as well, due to the acids in the lemon juice. If time allows, marinate the chops for slightly longer. Try other citrus juices in this recipe for a change. Both orange and lime juice would be delicious.

1 Trim the chops of any excess fat, wipe with a clean damp cloth and reserve. To make the marinade, using a pestle and mortar, pound the thyme leaves and rosemary with the salt until pulpy. Add the garlic and continue pounding until crushed. Stir in the lemon rind and juice and the olive oil.

2 Pour the marinade over the lamb chops, turning them until they are well coated. Cover lightly and leave to marinate in the refrigerator for about 1 hour.

3 Meanwhile, heat the oil in a large non-stick frying pan. Add the potatoes and garlic and cook over a low heat for about 20 minutes, stirring occasionally. Increase the heat and cook for a further 10–15 minutes until golden. Drain on absorbent kitchen paper and add salt to taste. Keep warm.

4 Heat a griddle pan until almost smoking. Add the lamb chops and cook for 3–4 minutes on each side until golden, but still pink in the middle. Serve with the potatoes, and either a mixed salad or freshly cooked vegetables.

Roasted Lamb with Rosemary & Garlic

INGREDIENTS

Serves 6

1.6 kg/3½ lb leg of lamb
8 garlic cloves, peeled
few sprigs of fresh rosemary
salt and freshly ground black pepper
4 slices pancetta
4 tbsp olive oil
4 tbsp red wine vinegar
900 g/2 lb potatoes
1 large onion
sprigs of fresh rosemary, to garnish
freshly cooked ratatouille, to serve

HELPFUL HINT

If you are unable to get a leg of lamb weighing exactly 1.6 kg/ 3½ lb, calculate the cooking time as follows: 20 minutes per 450 g/lb plus 30 minutes for rare, 25 minutes per 450 g/lb plus 30 minutes for medium and 30 minutes per 450 g/lb plus 30 minutes for well done.

1 Preheat oven to 200°C/400°F/Gas Mark 6, 15 minutes before roasting. Wipe the leg of lamb with a clean damp cloth, then place the lamb in a large roasting tin. With a sharp knife, make small, deep incisions into the meat.

2 Cut 2–3 garlic cloves into small slivers, then insert with a few small sprigs of rosemary into the lamb. Season to taste with salt and pepper and cover the lamb with the slices of pancetta.

3 Drizzle over 1 tablespoon of the olive oil and lay a few more rosemary sprigs across the lamb. Roast in the preheated oven for 30 minutes, then pour over the vinegar.

4 Peel the potatoes and cut into large dice. Peel the onion and cut into thick wedges then thickly slice the remaining garlic. Arrange around the lamb. Pour the remaining olive oil over the potatoes, then reduce the oven temperature to 180°C/350°F/Gas Mark 4 and roast for a further 1 hour, or until the lamb is tender. Garnish with fresh sprigs of rosemary and serve immediately with the roast potatoes and ratatouille.

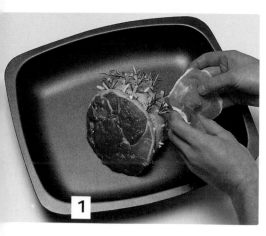

Braised Lamb with Broad Beans

INGREDIENTS

Serves 4

700 g/1½ lb lamb, cut into
   large chunks
1 tbsp plain flour
1 onion
2 garlic cloves
1 tbsp olive oil
400 g can chopped tomatoes
   with basil
300 ml/½ pint lamb stock
2 tbsp freshly chopped thyme
2 tbsp freshly chopped oregano
salt and freshly ground black pepper
150 g/5 oz frozen broad beans
fresh oregano, to garnish
creamy mashed potatoes, to serve

TASTY TIP

If you want to use fresh broad beans in season, you will need about 450 g/1 lb of beans in their pods for this recipe. If you prefer to peel the beans, plunge them first into boiling salted water for about 30 seconds, drain and refresh under cold water. The skins will come off very easily.

1. Trim the lamb, discarding any fat or gristle, then place the flour in a polythene bag, add the lamb and toss until coated thoroughly. Peel and slice the onion and garlic and reserve.

2. Heat the olive oil in a heavy-based saucepan and when hot, add the lamb and cook, stirring until the meat is sealed and browned all over. Using a slotted spoon transfer the lamb to a plate and reserve.

3. Add the onion and garlic to the saucepan and cook for 3 minutes, stirring frequently until softened, then return the lamb to the saucepan.

4. Add the chopped tomatoes with their juice, the stock, the chopped thyme and oregano to the pan and season to taste with salt and pepper. Bring to the boil, then cover with a close-fitting lid, reduce the heat and simmer for 1 hour.

5. Add the broad beans to the lamb and simmer for 20–30 minutes, or until the lamb is tender. Garnish with fresh oregano and serve with creamy mashed potatoes.

Lamb's Liver with Bacon & Onions

INGREDIENTS

Serves 4

350 g/12 oz lamb's liver
2 heaped tbsp plain flour
salt and freshly ground black pepper
2 tbsp groundnut oil
2 large onions, peeled and
  finely sliced
2 garlic cloves, peeled and chopped
1 red chilli, deseeded and chopped
175 g/6 oz streaky bacon
40 g/1½ oz butter
300 ml/½ pint lamb or beef stock
2 tbsp freshly chopped parsley

To serve:

freshly cooked creamy
  mashed potatoes
freshly cooked green vegetables
freshly cooked carrots

FOOD FACT

Groundnut or peanut oil is also known as arachide oil. It is often used in Thai cuisine because it is mild and almost flavourless and can be heated to a very high temperature without burning, which makes it perfect for stir-frying and deep-frying.

1 Trim the liver, discarding any sinew or tubes, and thinly slice. Season the flour with salt and pepper, then use to coat the liver. Reserve.

2 Heat a wok, then add the oil and when hot, add the sliced onion, garlic and chilli and cook for 5–6 minutes, or until soft and browned. Remove from the wok with a slotted spoon and reserve.

3 Cut each slice of the bacon in half and stir-fry for 3–4 minutes or until cooked. Remove with a slotted spoon and add to the onions.

4 Melt the butter in the wok and fry the liver on all sides until browned and crisp. Pour in the stock and allow to bubble fiercely for 1–2 minutes.

5 Return the onions and bacon to the wok, stir thoroughly, then cover. Simmer gently for 10 minutes, or until the liver is tender. Sprinkle with the parsley and serve immediately with mashed potatoes and green vegetables and carrots.

Pork Sausages with Onion Gravy & Best-ever Mash

INGREDIENTS

Serves 4

50 g/2 oz butter
1 tbsp olive oil
2 large onions, peeled and
  thinly sliced
pinch of sugar
1 tbsp freshly chopped thyme
1 tbsp plain flour
100 ml/3½ fl oz Madeira
200 ml/7 fl oz vegetable stock
8–12 good quality butchers pork
  sausages, depending on size

For the mash:

900 g/2 lb floury potatoes, peeled
75 g/3 oz butter
4 tbsp crème fraîche or soured cream
salt and freshly ground black pepper

HELPFUL HINT

There is a huge range of regional pork sausages to choose from. Try meaty Cambridge sausages packed with herbs and spices, or Cumberland sausages made form coarsely chopped pork and black pepper.

1 Melt the butter with the oil and add the onions. Cover and cook gently for about 20 minutes until the onions have collapsed. Add the sugar and stir well. Uncover and continue to cook, stirring often, until the onions are very soft and golden.

2 Add the thyme, stir well, then add the flour, stirring. Gradually add the Madeira and the stock. Bring to the boil and simmer gently for 10 minutes.

3 Meanwhile, put the sausages in a large frying pan and cook over a medium heat for about 15–20 minutes, turning often, until golden brown and slightly sticky all over.

4 For the mash, boil the potatoes in plenty of lightly salted water for 15–18 minutes until tender. Drain well and return to the saucepan. Put the saucepan over a low heat to allow the potatoes to dry thoroughly. Remove from the heat and add the butter, crème fraîche and salt and pepper. Mash thoroughly. Serve the potato mash topped with the sausages and onion gravy.

Roast Cured Pork Loin with Baked Sliced Potatoes

INGREDIENTS

Serves 4

2 tbsp wholegrain mustard

2 tbsp clear honey

1 tsp coarsely crushed black pepper

900 g/2 lb piece smoked cured
   pork loin

900 g/2 lb potatoes, peeled and
   thinly sliced

75 g/3 oz butter, diced

1 large onion, peeled and
   finely chopped

25 g/1 oz plain flour

salt and freshly ground black pepper

600 ml/1 pint milk

fresh green salad, to serve

HELPFUL HINT

Smoked cured pork loin can be found in specialist butchers and is delicately flavoured. If you are unable to find it, an ordinary piece of pork loin can be used here. It usually has a good layer of crackling, so remove it for this recipe, sprinkle with a little salt and cook separately under the grill.

1 Preheat the oven to 190°C/375°F/Gas Mark 5. Mix together the mustard, honey and black pepper. Spread evenly over the pork loin. Place in the centre of a large square of tinfoil and wrap loosely. Cook in the preheated oven for 15 minutes per 450 g/1 lb, plus an extra 15 minutes (45 minutes), unwrapping the joint for the last 30 minutes' cooking time.

2 Meanwhile, layer one-third of the potatoes, one-third of the butter, half the onions and half the flour in a large gratin dish. Add half the remaining potatoes and butter and the remaining onions and flour. Finally, cover with the remaining potatoes. Season well with salt and pepper between layers. Pour in the milk and dot with the remaining butter. Cover the dish loosely with tinfoil and put in the oven below the pork. Cook for 1½ hours.

3 Remove the tinfoil from the potatoes and cook for a further 20 minutes until tender and golden. Remove the pork loin from the oven and leave to rest for 10 minutes before carving thinly. Serve with the potatoes and a fresh green salad.

Oven-roasted Vegetables with Sausages

INGREDIENTS

Serves 4

2 medium aubergines, trimmed

3 medium courgettes, trimmed

4 tbsp olive oil

6 garlic cloves

8 Tuscan-style sausages

4 plum tomatoes

2 x 300 g cans cannellini beans

salt and freshly ground black pepper

1 bunch of fresh basil, torn into
    coarse pieces

4 tbsp Parmesan cheese, grated

1 Preheat oven to 200°C/400°F/Gas Mark 6, 15 minutes before cooking. Cut the aubergines and courgettes into bite-sized chunks. Place the olive oil in a large roasting tin and heat in the preheated oven for 3 minutes, or until very hot. Add the aubergines, courgettes and garlic cloves, then stir until coated in the hot oil and cook in the oven for 10 minutes.

2 Remove the roasting tin from the oven and stir. Lightly prick the sausages, add to the roasting tin and return to the oven. Continue to roast for a further 20 minutes, turning once during cooking, until the vegetables are tender and the sausages are golden brown.

3 Meanwhile, roughly chop the plum tomatoes and drain the cannellini beans. Remove the sausages from the oven and stir in the tomatoes and cannellini beans. Season to taste with salt and pepper, then return to the oven for 5 minutes, or until heated thoroughly.

4 Scatter over the basil leaves and sprinkle with plenty of Parmesan cheese and extra freshly ground black pepper. Serve immediately.

HELPFUL HINT

Although it is worth seeking out Tuscan-style sausages for this dish, a good alternative would be to use Toulouse sausages instead, as these are more readily available from large supermarkets and from selected butchers.

1

2

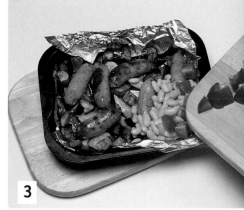

3

Pork Chop Hotpot

INGREDIENTS

Serves 4

4 pork chops
flour for dusting
225 g/8 oz shallots, peeled
2 garlic cloves, peeled
50 g/2 oz sun-dried tomatoes
2 tbsp olive oil
400 g can plum tomatoes
150 ml/¼ pint red wine
150 ml/¼ pint chicken stock
3 tbsp tomato purée
2 tbsp freshly chopped oregano
salt and freshly ground black pepper
fresh oregano leaves, to garnish

To serve:
freshly cooked new potatoes
French beans

1 Preheat oven to 190°C/375°F/Gas Mark 5, 10 minutes before cooking. Trim the pork chops, removing any excess fat, wipe with a clean, damp cloth, then dust with a little flour and reserve. Cut the shallots in half if large. Chop the garlic and slice the sun-dried tomatoes.

2 Heat the olive oil in a large casserole dish and cook the pork chops for about 5 minutes, turning occasionally during cooking, until browned all over. Using a slotted spoon, carefully lift out of the dish and reserve. Add the shallots and cook for 5 minutes, stirring occasionally.

3 Return the pork chops to the casserole dish and scatter with the garlic and sun-dried tomatoes, then pour over the can of tomatoes with their juice.

4 Blend the red wine, stock and tomato purée together and add the chopped oregano. Season to taste with salt and pepper, then pour over the pork chops and bring to a gentle boil. Cover with a close-fitting lid and cook in the preheated oven for 1 hour, or until the pork chops are tender. Adjust the seasoning to taste, then scatter with a few oregano leaves and serve immediately with freshly cooked potatoes and French beans.

TASTY TIP
Choose bone-in chops for this recipe. Remove any excess fat and rind before cooking.

Spaghetti & Meatballs

INGREDIENTS

Serves 4

400 g can chopped tomatoes
1 tbsp tomato paste
1 tsp chilli sauce
¼ tsp brown sugar
salt and freshly ground black pepper
350 g/12 oz spaghetti
75g/3 oz Cheddar cheese, grated,
  plus extra to serve
freshly chopped parsley, to garnish

For the meatballs:

450 g/1 lb lean pork or beef mince
125 g/4 oz fresh breadcrumbs
1 large onion, peeled and
  finely chopped
1 medium egg, beaten
1 tbsp tomato paste
2 tbsp freshly chopped parsley
1 tbsp freshly chopped oregano

TASTY TIP

For a crisper outside to the meatballs, you can fry them. Heat 2 tablespoons of olive oil in a very large frying pan and cook over a medium heat for about 15 minutes, turning occasionally, until well-browned.

1 Preheat the oven to 200°C/400°F/Gas Mark 6, 15 minutes before using. Place the chopped tomatoes, tomato paste, chilli sauce and sugar in a saucepan. Season to taste with salt and pepper and bring to the boil. Cover and simmer for 15 minutes, then cook, uncovered, for a further 10 minutes, or until the sauce has reduced and thickened.

2 Meanwhile, make the meatballs. Place the meat, breadcrumbs and onion in a food processor. Blend until all the ingredients are well mixed. Add the beaten egg, tomato paste, parsley and oregano and season to taste. Blend again.

3 Shape the mixture into small balls, about the size of an apricot, and place on an oiled baking tray. Cook in the preheated oven for 25–30 minutes, or until browned and cooked.

4 Meanwhile, bring a large pan of lightly salted water to a rolling boil. Add the pasta and cook according to the packet instructions, or until 'al dente'.

5 Drain the pasta and return to the pan. Pour over the tomato sauce and toss gently to coat the spaghetti. Tip into a warmed serving dish and top with the meatballs. Garnish with chopped parsley and serve immediately with grated cheese.

1

3

5

Cannelloni

INGREDIENTS

Serves 4

2 tbsp olive oil

175 g/6 oz fresh pork mince

75 g/3 oz chicken livers, chopped

1 small onion, peeled and chopped

1 garlic clove, peeled and chopped

175 g/6 oz frozen chopped
  spinach, thawed

1 tbsp freeze-dried oregano

pinch of freshly grated nutmeg

salt and freshly ground black pepper

175 g/6 oz ricotta cheese

25 g/1 oz butter

25 g/1 oz plain flour

600 ml/1 pint milk

600 ml/1 pint ready-made
  tomato sauce

16 precooked cannelloni tubes

50 g/2 oz Parmesan cheese, grated

green salad, to serve

TASTY TIP

To make chicken cannelloni, substitute 225 g/8 oz boneless, skinless chicken breast that has been finely chopped in a food processor. Minced chicken is also available from large supermarkets.

1 Preheat oven to 190°C/375°F/Gas Mark 5, 10 minutes before cooking. Heat the olive oil in a frying pan and cook the mince and chicken livers for about 5 minutes, stirring occasionally, until browned all over. Break up any lumps if necessary with a wooden spoon.

2 Add the onion and garlic and cook for 4 minutes, until softened. Add the spinach, oregano, nutmeg and season to taste with salt and pepper. Cook until all the liquid has evaporated, then remove the pan from the heat and allow to cool. Stir in the ricotta cheese.

3 Meanwhile, melt the butter in a small saucepan and stir in the plain flour to form a roux. Cook for 2 minutes, stirring occasionally. Remove from the heat and blend in the milk until smooth. Return to the heat and bring to the boil, stirring until the sauce has thickened. Reserve.

4 Spoon a thin layer of the tomato sauce on the base of a large ovenproof dish. Divide the pork filling between the cannelloni tubes. Arrange on top of the tomato sauce. Spoon over the remaining tomato sauce.

5 Pour over the white sauce and sprinkle with the Parmesan cheese. Bake in the preheated oven for 30–35 minutes, or until the cannelloni is tender and the top is golden brown. Serve immediately with a green salad.

Pork Meatballs with Vegetables

INGREDIENTS

Serves 4

450 g/1 lb pork mince
2 tbsp freshly chopped coriander
2 garlic cloves, peeled and chopped
1 tbsp light soy sauce
salt and freshly ground black pepper
2 tbsp groundnut oil
2 cm/1 inch piece fresh root ginger,
   peeled and cut into matchsticks
1 red pepper, deseeded and
   cut into chunks
1 green pepper, deseeded and cut
   into chunks
2 courgettes, trimmed and
   cut into sticks
125 g/4 oz baby sweetcorn,
   halved lengthways
3 tbsp light soy sauce
1 tsp sesame oil
fresh coriander leaves, to garnish
freshly cooked noodles, to serve

HELPFUL HINT

Chilling the meatballs firms and helps prevent them breaking up during cooking. If you find it easier, cook the pork balls in 2 batches.

1 Mix together the pork mince, the chopped coriander, half the garlic and the soy sauce, then season to taste with salt and pepper. Divide into 20 portions and roll into balls. Place on a baking sheet, cover with clingfilm and chill in the refrigerator for at least 30 minutes.

2 Heat a wok or large frying pan, add the groundnut oil and when hot, add the meatballs and cook for 8–10 minutes, or until the pork balls are browned all over, turning occasionally. Using a slotted spoon, transfer the balls to a plate and keep warm.

3 Add the ginger and remaining garlic to the wok and stir-fry for 30 seconds. Add the red and green peppers and stir-fry for 5 minutes. Add the courgettes and sweetcorn and stir-fry for 3 minutes.

4 Return the pork balls to the wok, add the soy sauce and sesame oil and stir-fry for 1 minute, until heated through. Garnish with coriander leaves and serve immediately on a bed of noodles.

Pork with Assorted Peppers

INGREDIENTS

Serves 4

450 g/1 lb pork fillet

2 tbsp groundnut oil

1 onion, peeled and thinly sliced

1 red pepper, deseeded and
cut into strips

1 yellow pepper, deseeded and cut
into strips

1 orange pepper, deseeded and cut
into strips

2 garlic cloves, peeled and crushed

2 tsp paprika

400 g can chopped tomatoes

300 ml/½ pint pork
or chicken stock

1 tsp soft dark brown sugar

salt and freshly ground black pepper

handful fresh oregano leaves

350 g/12 oz penne

2 tbsp grated mozzarella cheese

TASTY TIP

Fresh oregano has a fairly powerful flavour, very similar to that of marjoram. 1 teaspoon of dried oregano may be used if preferred.

1 Trim the pork fillet, discarding any sinew and fat, then cut into small cubes. Heat the wok, add the oil and, when hot, stir-fry the pork for 3–4 minutes until brown and sealed. Remove the pork from the wok and reserve.

2 Add the sliced onions to the wok and stir-fry until they are softened, but not browned, then add the pepper strips and stir-fry for a further 3–4 minutes.

3 Stir in the garlic, paprika, chopped tomatoes, stock, sugar and seasoning and bring to the boil. Simmer, uncovered, stirring occasionally, for 15 minutes, or until the sauce has reduced and thickened. Return the pork to the wok and simmer for a further 5–10 minutes. Sprinkle with the oregano leaves.

4 Cook the pasta for 3–4 minutes until 'al dente' or according to packet directions, then drain and serve immediately with the pork and grated mozzarella cheese.

Bacon, Mushroom & Cheese Puffs

INGREDIENTS

Serves 4

1 tbsp olive oil

225 g/8 oz field mushrooms, wiped
and roughly chopped

225 g/8 oz rindless streaky bacon,
roughly chopped

2 tbsp freshly chopped parsley

salt and freshly ground black pepper

350 g/12 oz ready-rolled puff pastry
sheets, thawed if frozen

25 g/1 oz Emmenthal cheese, grated

1 medium egg, beaten

salad leaves such as rocket or
watercress, to garnish

tomatoes, to serve

TASTY TIP

The Emmenthal cheese in this recipe can be substituted for any other cheese, but for best results use a cheese such as Cheddar, which like Emmenthal melts easily! The bacon can also be substituted for slices of sweeter cured hams such as pancetta, speck, Parma or prosciutto.

1 Preheat the oven to 200°C/400°F/Gas Mark 6. Heat the olive oil in a large frying pan.

2 Add the mushrooms and bacon and fry for 6–8 minutes until golden in colour. Stir in the parsley, season to taste with salt and pepper and allow to cool.

3 Roll the sheet of pastry a little thinner on a lightly floured surface to a 30.5 cm/12 inch square. Cut the pastry into 4 equal squares.

4 Stir the grated Emmenthal cheese into the mushroom mixture. Spoon a quarter of the mixture on to one half of each square.

5 Brush the edges of the square with a little of the beaten egg.

6 Fold over the pastry to form a triangular parcel. Seal the edges well and place on a lightly oiled baking sheet. Repeat until the squares are done.

7 Make shallow slashes in the top of the pastry with a knife.

8 Brush the parcels with the remaining beaten egg and cook in the preheated oven for 20 minutes, or until puffy and golden brown.

9 Serve warm or cold, garnished with the salad leaves and served with tomatoes.

2

4

7

Step-by-Step, Practical Recipes Meat Eats: Tips & Hints

Helpful Hint

Dry-frying spices really releases their flavour. It is a particularly good way to flavour lean meat, such as chicken or lamb. Try mixing dry-fried spices with a little water or oil to make a paste. Spread the paste on the meat before baking to make a spicy crust.

Helpful Hint

It is important that you get the temperature of the oil right. If you do not have a thermometer, drop a small cube of bread into the hot oil; if it turns crisp and golden in 30 seconds the oil is ready.

Food Fact

Tomatoes are such an integral part of many cuisines that it is hard to believe they were only introduced to Europe from the Americas a few hundred years ago. There are lots of new flavoursome varieties now available that complement meat dishes excellently. Those sold still attached to the vine tend to have particularly good flavour.

Helpful Hint

Best-end-of-neck lamb consists of 6–7 small chops. A crown roast of lamb is made by joining two best ends of lamb neck together, making a perfect central cavity to fill with stuffing. When ready to serve, the trimmed cutlet bones may be topped, if liked with paper frills, looking like tiny chef's hats.

Tasty Tip

When choosing a cut of steak, choose a thick cut over a thin one. Thick cuts of steak of an inch thick or more can develop a beautiful crust without drying out the insides unnecessarily.

Helpful Hint

Avoid bulk buying meat where possible, unless buying for the freezer. Fresh foods lose their nutritional value rapidly, so buying a little at a time minimises loss of nutrients. It also reduces the risk of a packed refrigerator, which reduces the effectiveness of the refrigeration process.

Helpful Hint

Do not reheat food more than once. If using a microwave, always check that the food is piping hot all the way through. The food should reach 70°C/158°F and needs to be cooked at that temperature for at least three minutes to ensure that all bacteria are killed.

Tasty Tip

The best joints for roast beef are a Rib of Beef, a Sirloin or a Fillet. Rib works well as it is usually cooked on the bone and the bone makes for a tastier piece of beef when cooked, but both Sirloin and Fillet are also very good.

Helpful Hint

It is important to store meat correctly once purchased from a butcher or supermarket. At home unwrap your meat, loosely cover it and store it on the bottom shelf of the fridge. Keep fresh chicken and pork for 2 days; beef and lamb will keep fresh for 4 days. Small cuts such as stewing steak, liver and mince should be used on the day you buy them or the following day. During this storage time, remember to change the dish the meat is on every day. Meat can spoil if it is left standing in blood or liquid. Always make sure your fridge is cold enough. A temperature of between 0°C and 2°C is best.

Tasty Tip

Before roasting any joint of meat, especially lamb and beef, take it out of the fridge and let it sit for 30 minutes. A joint at room temperature will roast more evenly. Also, using a roasting rack will ensure even browning and heat circulation.

Helpful Hint

There are many oven-based recipes that can easily be adapted to be cooked on a barbecue, which is a healthy way to cook meat, as long as it is cooked thoroughly. It is sometimes preferable to finish some meats off in the oven to achieve even cooking. When cooking meat on a barbecue, it is important to remember that meat needs to sear and also to cook slowly to absorb smoke. So always put coals on only one side, so you have a grill with two different temperatures. One side is for attaining a crust whilst the other is for cooking the meat to a juicy, tender interior.

First published in 2013 by
FLAME TREE PUBLISHING LTD
Crabtree Hall, Crabtree Lane, Fulham,
London, SW6 6TY, United Kingdom
www.flametreepublishing.com

The CIP record for this book is available from the British Library • Printed in China

NOTE: Recipes using uncooked eggs should be avoided by infants, the elderly, pregnant women and anyone suffering from an illness.

18 17 16 15 14 13   10 9 8 7 6 5 4 3 2 1

ISBN: 978-0-85775-857-6

ACKNOWLEDGEMENTS: Authors: Catherine Atkinson, Juliet Barker, Gina Steer, Vicki Smallwood, Carol Tennant, Mari Mererid Williams, Elizabeth Wolf-Cohen and Simone Wright. Photography: Colin Bowling, Paul Forrester and Stephen Brayne. Home Economists and Stylists: Jacqueline Bellefontaine, Mandy Phipps, Vicki Smallwood and Penny Stephens. All props supplied by Barbara Stewart at Surfaces. Publisher and Creative Director: Nick Wells. Editorial: Catherine Taylor, Laura Bulbeck, Esme Chapman and Emma Chafer. Design and Production: Chris Herbert, Mike Spender and Helen Wall.